Grade Boosters

BOOSTING YOUR WAY TO SUCCESS IN SCHOOL

First Grade Math

By Zondra Lewis Knapp

Illustrated by Dave C. Lowe

Lowell House
Juvenile
Los Angeles

CONTEMPORARY BOOKS
Chicago

To Drea and David, the ultimate Grade Boosters . . .
—Z.L.K.

About the Author

Zondra "Zee" Knapp holds a Masters of Education in curriculum development, a Masters of Arts in school management, and a Ph.D. in administration. She is a curriculum writing specialist with the California Department of Education, judge for the California Science Fair and Orange County Science and Engineering Fair, and a National Aeronautics and Space Administration NEWMAST Mentor Teacher.

Publisher: Jack Artenstein
General Manager, Juvenile Division: Elizabeth D. Amos
Project Editor: Lisa Melton
Text Design: Carolyn Wendt

Manufactured in the United States of America

ISBN: 1-56565-375-0

10 9 8 7 6 5 4 3 2 1

Lowell House books can be purchased at special discounts when ordered in bulk for premiums and special sales. Contact Department JH at the following address:

Lowell House Juvenile
2029 Century Park East
Suite 3290
Los Angeles, CA 90067

BOOSTING SUCCESS IN MATH

GRADE BOOSTERS: First Grade Math is an innovative book designed to help boost your child's success in developing math skills, together with critical and creative thinking skills, *at a young age.* Armed with these abilities, your child will be prepared to meet academic challenges throughout his or her education.

By building math literacy and self-esteem through age- and grade-appropriate activities, **GRADE BOOSTERS: First Grade Math** develops the basic math skills necessary for further learning. The clever exercises not only teach and reinforce critical and creative thinking skills, but they also encourage your child to explore the mathematical concepts present in everyday life. Skills include classifying objects and shapes, identifying and manipulating numbers and patterns, practicing hand-eye tracking, interpreting clues, organizing data, and reaching conclusions through reasoning. Moreover, because it is highly visual, **GRADE BOOSTERS: First Grade Math** is ideal for both native English-speaking children, as well as those learning English as a second language who may need a "boost" in their basic math skills.

How to Use This Book

GRADE BOOSTERS: First Grade Math offers your child a vast variety of opportunities to learn about math. The book is divided into different mathematical sections, as indicated by the headline in the upper left- or right-hand corners. Each new section begins with a listing of "My New Math Words." Then, a series of playful, skill-building activities helps your child learn that concept. When a new section appears, your child will also be able to review material already learned, in "My Old Math Words."

The Skills list at the bottom of the page indicates exactly which skills are being developed on that page.

Ending each section are "Let's Review," which checks your child's progress on mastering concepts, and an achievement award, which helps develop a sense of academic accomplishment. This recognition gives your child a feeling of success in mathematics and promotes self-esteem. Encourage your child to put these awards in a special place where your family can recognize your child's accomplishments.

Two additional features also appear throughout **GRADE BOOSTERS: First Grade Math.** TOGETHER TIME, designed especially for interactive learning, offers math activities for you and your child to enjoy together.

Note to Parents

These home-school extensions provide a valuable opportunity for you to help strengthen your child's math skills. Because you do the activities together, your child will also develop a sense of the importance of math that he or she will carry throughout life. Finally, the GRADE BOOSTER! feature enriches and extends your child's basic math skills by providing critical- and creative-thinking exercises.

Time Spent Together

The time you spend with your child as he or she learns is invaluable. Therefore, the more positive and constructive an environment you can create, the better. In working together, allow your child the freedom to go at his or her own pace. If your child would like to talk about the pictures, and freely share and express opinions, all the better. Ask questions about what your child sees. Be creative! Encourage your child to predict actions or events, or even make up a story about what he or she sees on the page.

Although the book closely follows the sequence many first grade teachers use throughout the country, you can start anywhere. Remember to consider your child's ability. Because the activities range from easy to more difficult, you may need to work with your child on many of the pages. Read the directions and explain them. Go over the examples that are given. While creativity should be encouraged and praised, help your child look for the best answer.

Work together only as long as your child remains interested. If necessary, practice a single section or page at a time. Then, before going on to a new section, review work just completed. That will ensure better recall of concepts. Remember that eagerness, willingness, and success are much more important in the long run than exactness or perfection. Remember, too, that your child's level of participation will vary at different times. Sometimes a response may be very brief and simplistic; at other times, a response may be elaborate and creative. Allow room for both. Much more learning will take place in a secure, accepting environment.

Positive experiences promote positive attitudes—a desire to learn and curiosity about the world. You can be an instrumental tool in helping your child develop a positive attitude toward learning. Your "one-to-one" contact cannot be duplicated at school. Therefore, you have a choice opportunity to share with your child as he or she learns about the world.

This book belongs to . . .

_____

My first name   My middle name   My last name

_____

My address number   My street   My apartment
                                                number

_____

My city   My state   My zip code

(   )
_____

My area code   My phone number

I already know a lot about my math. Now I am going to learn more!

MY NEW MATH WORDS: About Amounts

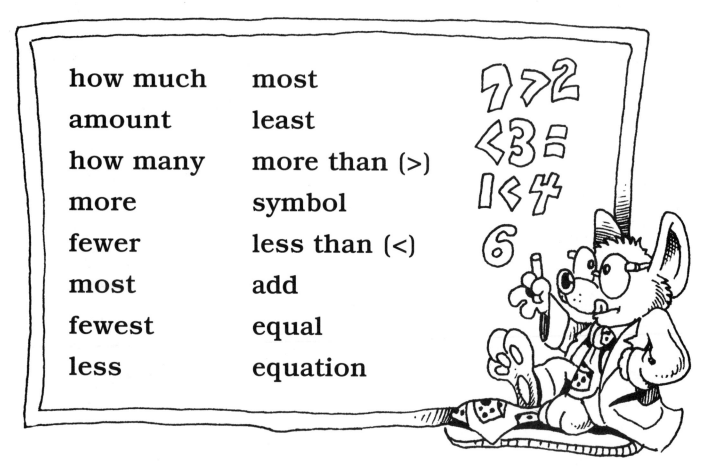

how much	most
amount	least
how many	more than (>)
more	symbol
fewer	less than (<)
most	add
fewest	equal
less	equation

What is a "math word"? It is any word that has to do with math! Now that you are in first grade, you probably know a lot of math words. Can you think of a few that are not listed above?

Write them here:

_____

_____

Skills: math literacy, vocabulary building, words associated with numbers

When we talk about **how much** we have of something, we are talking about **amount**. How much hot chocolate do you see?

When we talk about **how many** we have of something, we are also talking about amount. How many apples do you see?

Take a quick look at the two bags below. Guess how many bears are in each bag. Write your guess on the blank lines.

My guess: _____   My guess: _____

Skills: estimating amounts, how much and how many

Now go back and count how many bears are in each bag. Were your guesses right?

Which holds **more** bears, BAG A or BAG B? _____

Which holds **fewer** bears, BAG A or BAG B? _____

Now it's time for some jelly beans! Which pan on the balance scale holds the **most** jelly beans, Pan 1 or Pan 2? Which holds the **fewest**? Write MOST or FEWEST on the blank lines.

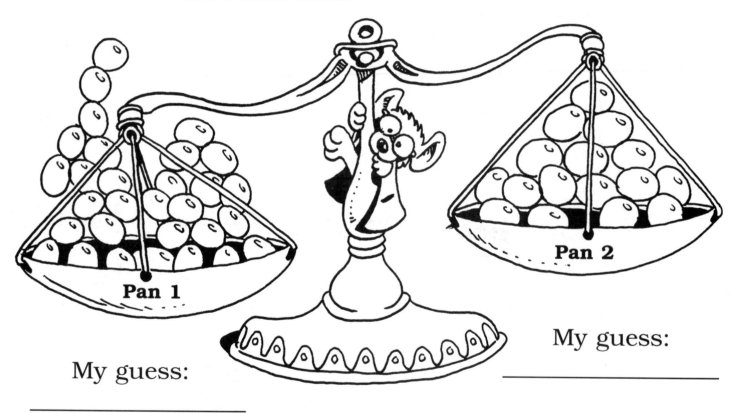

Pan 1

Pan 2

My guess:

_____

My guess:

_____

Count up the jelly beans now. Pan 1 holds _____ jelly beans. Pan 2 holds _____ jelly beans. Did you guess MOST and FEWEST correctly?

Skills: estimating amounts, inference, more and fewer, most and fewest

Quick! Guess whose bucket holds **more** water, Sam's or Kathy's? Put a ✓ next to the bucket that holds more water. Put an X next to the bucket that holds **less** water.

Who has more popcorn, Tina or Sal? Put a ✓ next to the tub that holds the **most** popcorn. Mark an X next to the tub with the **least** amount.

GRADE BOOSTER!

Which words belong together? Circle the words that belong with MORE. Underline the words that belong with LESS.

| most | least | fewer | greatest |
| lesser | few | greater | less |

Help Monty decide which branch has more bananas on it. One has 7 bananas on it. The other has 5.

7 is **more than** **5**

Sometimes we write *more than* with a **symbol** (a picture) that looks like this: >. On the line below, write the math symbol that means *more than*.

7 _____ **5**

TOGETHER TIME: Here's a cereal game to play with your mom, dad, or a friend: Wash your hands, spread out some napkins, then each of you pull out a handful of cereal and put it on a napkin. Count the cereal pieces. Who has more? Write the math symbol > and the numbers on a piece of paper. Use raisins or candy and play again!

Skills: counting, more than, math symbols

Monty and his friend Manuel have eaten a lot of bananas! Count up the banana peels, then write the missing numbers on the lines in the box. Who has eaten more bananas?

_____ is more than _____

Write in the missing math symbol on the line:

7 _____ 4

GRADE BOOSTER!

See if you can put together what you have learned so far. It's easy! Just fill in 3 math symbols that mean more than.

10 ___ 7 ___ 5 ___ 4

Henrietta Hen has fewer eggs in one basket than in another. Point to the basket that holds less.

6	is **less than**	**7**

Sometimes we write *less than* using this symbol: <. On the line below, write the math symbol that means *less than*.

6 _____ **7**

Now count up the decorated eggs. Then fill in the missing numbers and math symbol to the right!

_____ is less than _____
(number)   (number)

_____   _____   _____
(number)   (symbol)   (number)

Skills: counting, less than, math symbols

Blue Sky, a Navajo girl, is watching some number-clouds in the sky! For each pair of numbers, draw a circle around the number that is more.

Blue Sky's brother, Falling Star, is watching the number-clouds, too. In each pair, circle the number that is less.

Here's a tough one! Which row in the rug has more feathers in it? Circle which one: TOP   BOTTOM. How many more feathers does this row have? _____

Now, point to the row that has less. How many less? _____ How many feathers would you need to **add** to this row to make it **equal** to (the same as) the other row? _____

When you put numbers and symbols together to figure out a problem, you are writing an **equation**. Finish the equation!

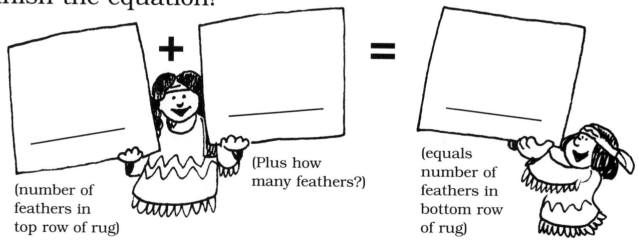

(number of feathers in top row of rug)

(Plus how many feathers?)

(equals number of feathers in bottom row of rug)

Skills: addition, subtraction, math symbols, writing equations

LET'S REVIEW

Now take a little test to see how much you have learned about amounts. Look at Snappy and Squiggly. The two squirrels have gathered some acorns and leaves.

1. How many ⬤'s does Snappy have? _____
How many ⬤'s does Squiggly have? _____

Write an equation using the > symbol: ___ > ___

2. How many 🍂's does Snappy have? _____
How many 🍂's does Squiggly have? _____

Write an equation using the < symbol: ___ < ___

3. How many ⬤'s *and* 🍂's does each squirrel have?
Snappy's total: _____ Squiggly's total: _____

Write an equation using > or < ! _____ _____

The Award
for the
MOST Wonderful
Mathematician
Goes to:

_____
(my name)

How many do you see on the page?

's _____   's _____

's _____   's _____

Which one is the most? _____
Which one is the least? _____
Are there any with the same number?
Which ones? _____

_____

MY NEW MATH WORDS:
About Sizes & Shapes

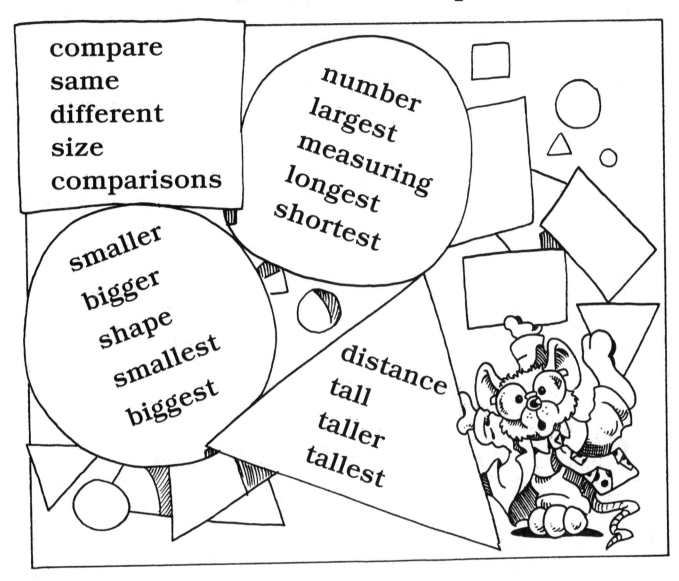

compare
same
different
size
comparisons

number
largest
measuring
longest
shortest

smaller
bigger
shape
smallest
biggest

distance
tall
taller
tallest

MY OLD MATH WORDS

Practice your old math words by writing the numbers where they belong. The first one is done for you.

(3, 11)   (11, 3)   (24, 3, 21)

3 > 11   __ < __   __ + __ = __

Skills: math literacy, vocabulary building, words associated with sizes and shapes

Size & Shape Comparisons

When you **compare** objects, you look to see how they are the **same** or how they are **different**. There are lots of ways to compare objects. Let's make some *size comparisons*.

Pug and Gogg are the same size.

Stump and James are not the same size. Stump is **smaller**, and James is **bigger**.

Pug   Gogg   Stump   James

In each box, two monsters are the same size. Circle them.

Skills: making comparisons, size, sameness

Size isn't the only thing you can compare.

These prints have
the same **shape**.

These have a
different shape.

Two pictures in each box are the same size *and* shape.
Draw a ◯ around the ones that are the same.

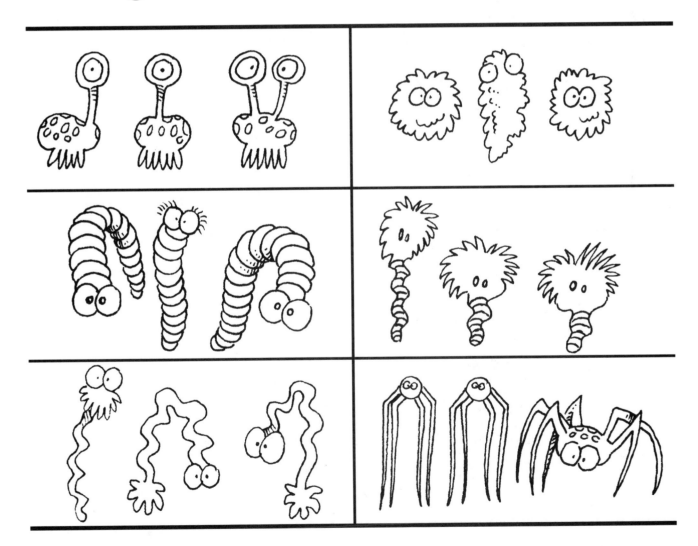

GRADE BOOSTER!

Here's a tough one. Put a ✔ beside the two bunnies that are the same size and shape.

Sammy is juggling three balls. The **smallest** one is above his nose! Help Sammy put a ◯ around the smallest picture in each box below.

Skills: making comparisons, size, sameness, sequencing sizes from smallest to biggest

Which is the **biggest** bug that Brenda Badger is holding? Help Brenda put a ⌒ around the biggest picture in each row.

GRADE BOOSTER!

*Look at the 8 pawprints. They are all nearly the same shape, but they are different in size. Can you **number** the pawprints from smallest to **largest** (biggest)?*

Here's how you do it:

1. Find the smallest .

2. Put a "1" inside the ◯ of that 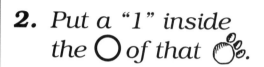.

3. Then find the next biggest 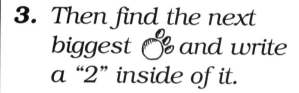 and write a "2" inside of it.

4. Where is the next biggest 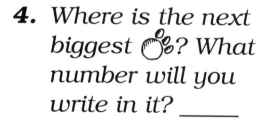? What number will you write in it? _____

5. What number will you put in the last ? _____

Skills: sequencing sizes from smallest to largest using numbers, visual discrimination

Sammy and Brenda are **measuring** elephants. They are the same shape but different sizes.

Now you can show Brenda and Sammy what *you* know about sizes. With your pencil, trace the smallest picture, then draw the other two sizes on your own! The first one is done for you.

SMALLEST	BIGGER	BIGGEST	SMALLEST	BIGGER	BIGGEST
△	△	△	◯		
☐			☐		
◯			♡		

Size & Shape Comparisons

Gary the Gorilla wants to buy some new clothes.
Which pair of pants below is the **longest**?
Circle which pair: 1st   2nd   3rd
Are those too long for Gary? YES NO
Which pair is just right?   1st   2nd   3rd

Now Gary needs a belt. Which belt is the **shortest**?
Circle which belt: 1st   2nd   3rd
Is that belt too short for Gary? YES NO
Which belt is just right?   1st   2nd   3rd

Skills: length comparisons, matching length, following directions, ordinal numbers

Sammy Snake loves to draw pictures that are long. Help him draw a ⟳ around the musical instrument that is the longest. Mark an X over the shortest.

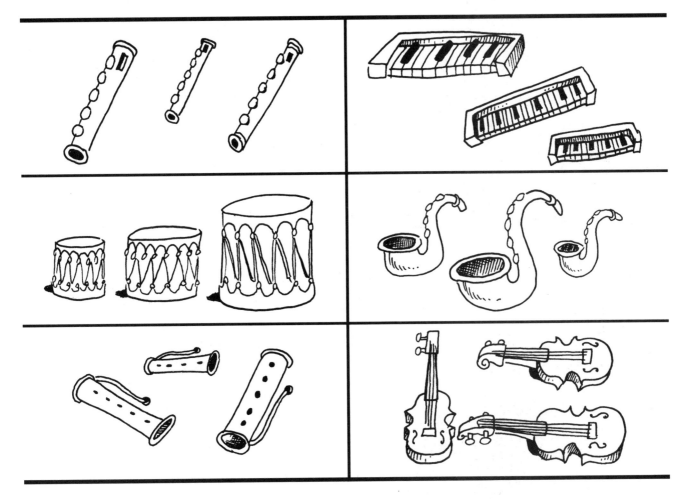

TOGETHER TIME: You can make some fun prints with a friend. Get some paper and pencils. Draw around your hand (both of you). Whose hand is longest? Whose is shortest? Now trace and measure your feet!

Skills: length comparisons—long, short, longest, shortest

What do you think? Read each question and guess the answer.

Which is longer, your head or your foot?

Which is a longer **distance**, from your belly button to your knees, or from your belly button to the top of your head?

Which is a longer distance, from the tips of your fingers to your elbow, or from your knee to the tips of your toes?

TOGETHER TIME: Ask your mom, dad, or other adult friend to use a measuring tape to help you measure the distances in the questions above. (If a measuring tape is not available, use a piece of string to compare distances.) Were you correct? Happy measuring!

Stretchy Swan has drawn some **tall** pictures with her crayons. Can you finish the **taller** and **tallest** pictures in the boxes by tracing over them?

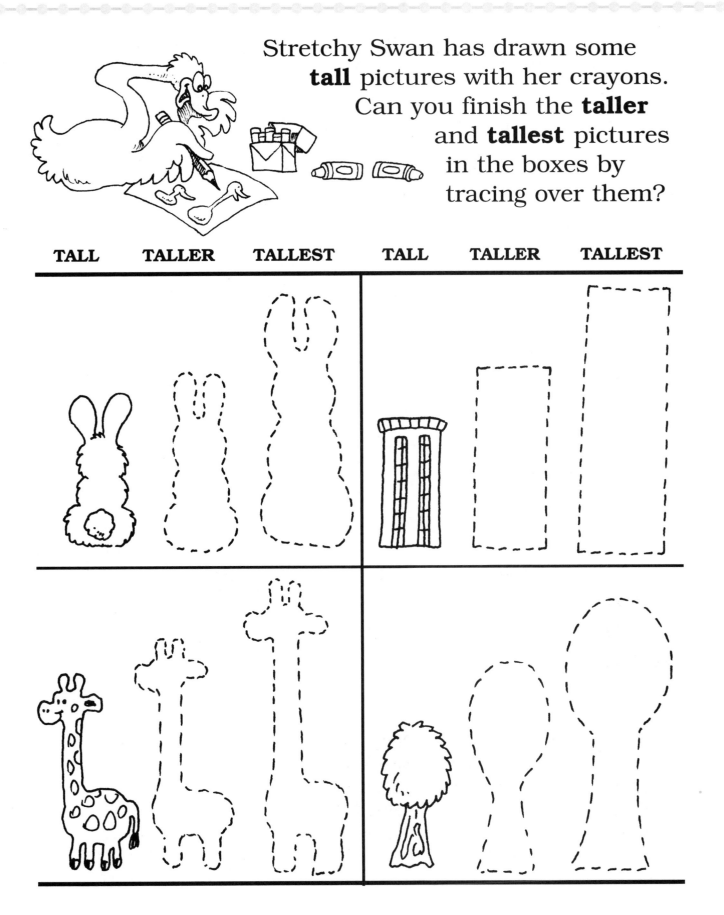

| TALL | TALLER | TALLEST | TALL | TALLER | TALLEST |

Skills: height comparisons, sequencing tall to tallest, hand-eye coordination, visual discrimination

GRADE BOOSTER!

Draw pictures of some of the people in your family! Make sure to get the sizes right. For instance, put the tallest person in your family in the "TALLEST" picture frame.

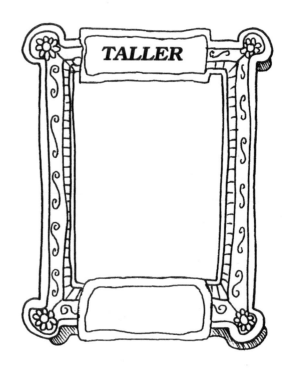

Be sure to fill in your family members' names at the bottom of each picture!

Skills: height comparisons, sequencing tall to tallest, using mathematics to solve everyday problems

LET'S REVIEW

Here's Mr. Mouse's family! Help him compare the sizes of his family members.

1. One mouse is the tallest. Color him green.

2. The biggest mouse gets to be red.

3. Color the mouse who is the shortest blue.

4. Two mice have a different shape than the others. Draw an X next to these.

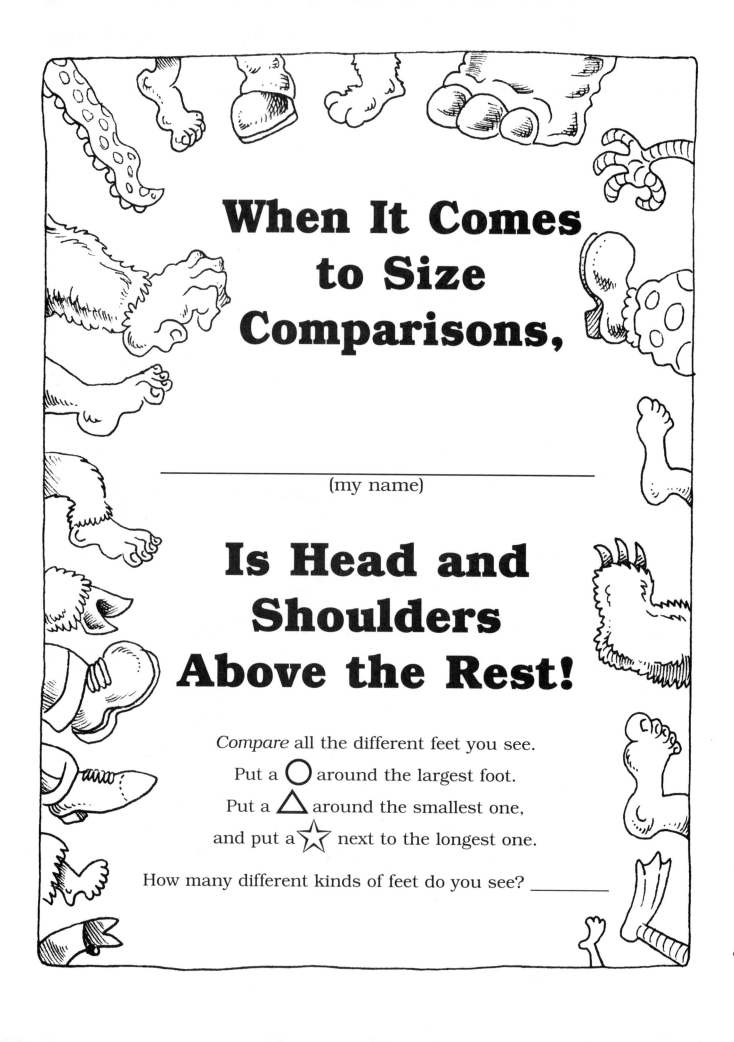

When It Comes to Size Comparisons,

_____

(my name)

Is Head and Shoulders Above the Rest!

Compare all the different feet you see.

Put a ◯ around the largest foot.

Put a △ around the smallest one,

and put a ☆ next to the longest one.

How many different kinds of feet do you see? _____

MY NEW MATH WORDS:
About Addition & Subtraction

addition

plus sign (+)

all

add

total

sum

equal sign (=)

addition problem

subtraction

minus sign (–)

subtract

difference

subtraction problem

table

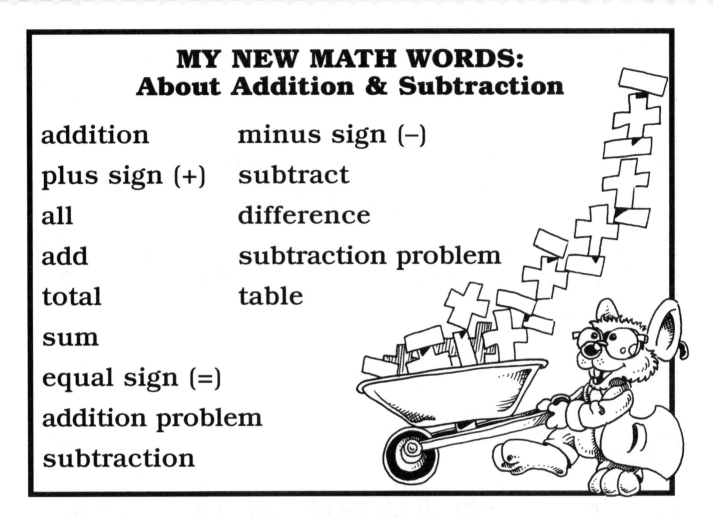

MY OLD MATH WORDS

Compare the shapes of these clowns. Which one is big? Which is small? Which one is short and which one tall? Draw a line from the old math word to its picture.

big   small   short   tall

Putting numbers together is called **addition**. The picture symbol used for addition is called a **plus sign (+)**. Look at the pictures below, then answer the questions using addition!

Three bears are jumping rope.   Two more come to play.

How many bears were jumping rope? _____
How many more bears came to play? _____
How many bears are there in **all**? **Add** them: _____

When you add two numbers together, you get a **total**, or **sum**. The picture symbol used for a total is an **equal sign (=)**. Here is your "beary" **addition problem**:

$$3 \text{ 🐻's} + 2 \text{ 🐻's} = 5 \text{ 🐻's}$$

Skills: addition, math symbols, equations

Now try this Piggy problem!
Pretend your friend gave you four
pennies for Piggy, your bank.

Then your dad gave you
three more pennies.

How many pennies did your friend give you? _____
How many more pennies did your dad give you? _____
How many pennies do you have in all? Add them: _____

The equation for this addition problem looks like this:

4 + 3 = 7
Out loud, you would say:
"Four plus three equals seven."

GRADE BOOSTER!

1

*Bernice has gathered some carrots,
turnips, and lettuce. Write the total
for each vegetable on the
lines below. How many
vegetables are there in all?*

____ + ____ + ____ = ____

TOGETHER TIME! To play this game called "Fish," you will need a carton of goldfish crackers, some paper, a pencil, and a paper plate. You can play with your mom, dad, some friends—anyone you wish!

Here's how you play: The first player throws some fish crackers onto the paper plate and counts them. Then the first player writes down the number on a piece of paper.

The second player throws in some more goldfish, counts how many more, then writes down the number on the same piece of paper.

Then the first player (or a third player) adds the two amounts and writes down the total after the equal sign in the equation.

4 + 2 = 6

Take turns starting each new game. When you're through playing, have a nice snack!

Skills: addition, math symbols, math games, writing equations, word problems

Now that you know how to add numbers together, you are ready to take numbers away. That is called **subtraction**. The symbol used for subtraction is a **minus sign (–)**. Look at the pictures below.

Six silly green frogs were sitting on six water lily pads.

A big bird flew by and two jumped off into the water.

How many frogs were sitting on the lily pads? _____
How many frogs jumped off? _____
How many frogs were left? **Subtract** them: _____

When you subtract one number from another, you get the **difference**. Here is your "froggy" **subtraction problem**:

$$6 \text{'s} - 2 \text{'s} = 4 \text{'s}$$

Four hungry cats
went on a picnic.

Two cats spotted
some mice and took
off to catch them!

How many cats went on the picnic? _____
How many cats ran after the mice? _____
How many cats were left? _____

Now write the missing numbers in this subtraction
problem:

4 **–** ___ **=** ___

Out loud, you would say:
"Four minus _____ equals _____."

TOGETHER TIME! Ask your mom, dad, or a friend to
gather 10 pennies, then change the cat story above.
Example: Put 1 penny on each cat, then take 3 pennies
away. Do you get the same answer as you did above?
Then put two pennies on each cat and take 4 away.
What answer do you get this time?

Skills: subtraction, math symbols, writing equations, word problems

Benjamin Bunny likes to hippy-hop across the numbers. Can you help him fill in the missing numbers by adding?

Adding one's:

0 1 2 3 4 5 __ __ __ __ __
+1 +1 +1 +1 +1 +1   +1   +1   +1   +1

Adding two's:

0 2 4 6 8 10 __ __ __ __ __
+2 +2 +2 +2 +2 +2   +2   +2   +2   +2

Adding three's:

0 3 6 9 12 __ __ __ __
+3 +3 +3 +3 +3   +3   +3   +3

Now help Benjamin fill in the blanks by subtracting.

Subtracting one's:

10 9 8 7 6 5 __ __ __ __ __
−1 −1 −1 −1 −1 −1   −1   −1   −1   −1

Subtracting two's:

20 18 16 14 12 10 __ __ __ __ __
−2 −2 −2 −2 −2 −2   −2   −2   −2   −2

Subtracting three's:

21 18 15 12 __ __ __ __
−3 −3 −3 −3   −3   −3   −3

Adding & Subtracting

Angela Alligator is playing an addition game. You can play, too. Fill up the **table** using the same pattern of X's and O's.

X	O	X	O	X
X		X		X
	O		O	

Help Angela count the total number of X's: _____
Count the total number of O's: _____
Now add (+) the total number of X's and O's together!
Write the sum on the line: _____

Skills: addition, math games, sequencing patterns, word patterns

Angela Alligator is not certain how to write down an equation for her addition problem of X's and O's. Could you help her? You know what to do! First write the numbers in the blanks:

___ **X**'s **+** ___ **O**'s **=** ___

Now fill in the numbers *and* the symbols. You can do it —it's easy!

_____ (symbol)   _____ (symbol)

_____ (number)   _____ (number)   _____ (total number)

GRADE BOOSTER!

Here are three more fun shapes to add up. Write an equation to show how many shapes there are in all.

____ O's + ____ 🌸's + ____ ✦'s = ____ *shapes*

Here is a subtraction game you can help Oliver Opossum play. You and Oliver have 25¢ to buy some of these toys.

When you buy a toy, put an X over it, then write it down in the table. The first toy is crossed out for you. It costs 4¢, so now you have only 21¢ left. That is your new total. Each time you buy a toy, subtract it until you have *no more money* to spend.

25¢	–	4¢	=	21¢
21¢	–	___¢	=	___¢
___¢	–	___¢	=	___¢
___¢	–	___¢	=	___¢
___¢	–	___¢	=	___¢
___¢	–	___¢	=	___¢

Skills: subtraction, money facts, problem solving, critical thinking

It's time to be an author! An author is a person who makes up stories. You can make up your own math story about adding and subtracting numbers. Be sure to use the plus (+), minus (–), and equals (=) signs in your story. Use another sheet of paper if you need to.

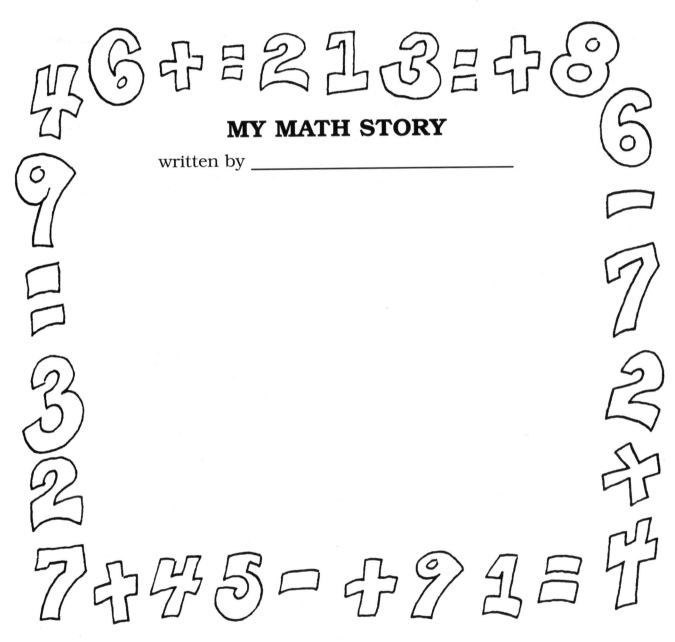

MY MATH STORY

written by _____

When you are done writing your story, draw a picture about it, then tell the story to your best friend!

Skills: creative writing and illustrating, using addition and subtraction equations

LET'S REVIEW

1. In this little test, match an elf on the left with an elf on the right. (Hint: each symbol goes with a word).

2. Now write the missing math symbol that will make each of the equations below correct.

5	__	1	=	6
5	+	1	__	6
3	__	2	=	1
5	__	4	__	1
8	__	2	__	10

Skills: comprehension, addition, subtraction, writing equations, deductive reasoning

SUPER MATH AWARD!

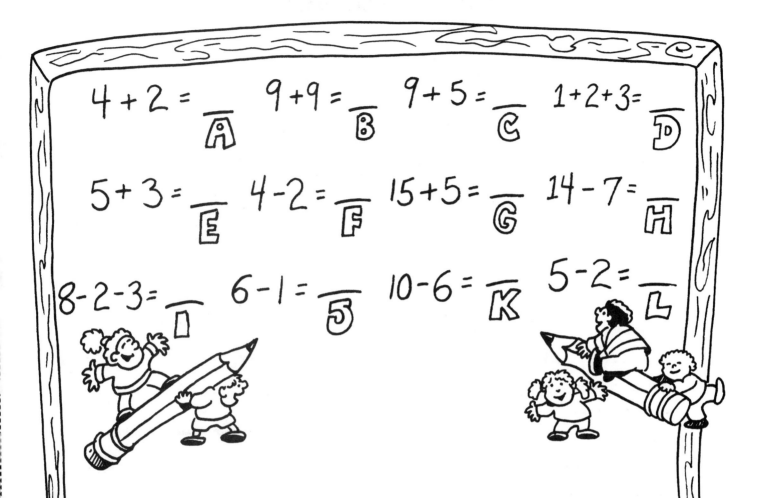

$4 + 2 =$ ___ A $9 + 9 =$ ___ B $9 + 5 =$ ___ C $1+2+3 =$ ___ D

$5 + 3 =$ ___ E $4 - 2 =$ ___ F $15 + 5 =$ ___ G $14 - 7 =$ ___ H

$8-2-3 =$ ___ I $6 - 1 =$ ___ J $10 - 6 =$ ___ K $5 - 2 =$ ___ L

_____
(my name)

Can *Add* (+) and *Subtract* (−) Numbers!

After completing the addition and subtractions problem above, use the answers you get to do the math problems below!

J + A = _____   G − I = _____   K + C = _____

E − D = _____   F + L = _____   B − H = _____

MY NEW MATH WORDS:
About Graphing

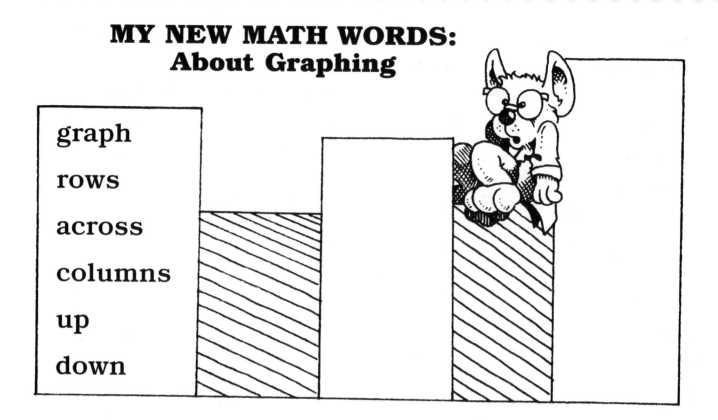

graph

rows

across

columns

up

down

MY OLD MATH WORDS

Can you put all the equations in the right basket? Use a solid line for the addition problems and a dashed line for the subtraction problems. The first one is done for you.

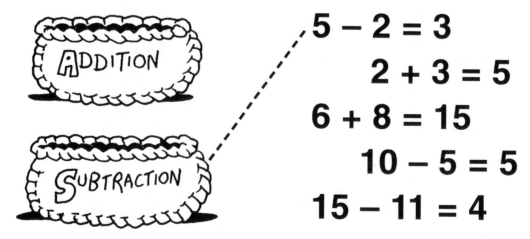

$5 - 2 = 3$

$2 + 3 = 5$

$6 + 8 = 15$

$10 - 5 = 5$

$15 - 11 = 4$

One math equation is incorrect! Circle it.

Skills: math literacy, vocabulary building, words associated with graphing

Geoffrey and Georgia Giraffe love to make graphs. What do you suppose a **graph** is?

A graph has **rows** of squares. A row goes **across**.

A graph has **columns** of squares, too. A column goes **up** and **down**.

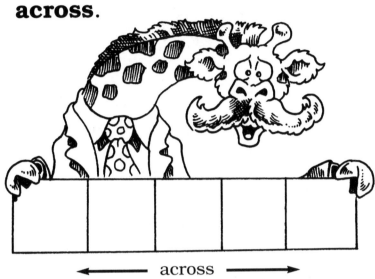

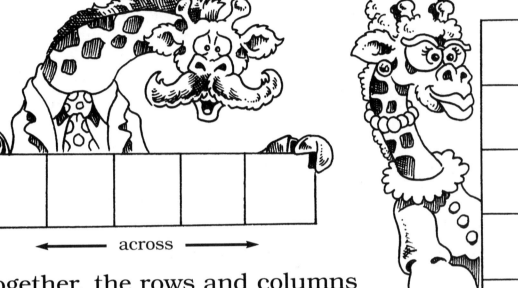

◄——— across ———►

up
and
down

Together, the rows and columns make a graph that looks like this:

	column 1	column 2	column 3	column 4
row 4				
row 3				
row 2				
row 1				

Skills: graphing, rows and columns, linear relationships

Now you can get started
on making your very own graph.

Here is a happy face:

Here is a sad face:

Count up the happy and sad faces you see below,
then answer the questions at the bottom of the page.

How many ☺'s did you count? _____
How many ☹'s did you count? _____
How many faces are there in all? _____

Skills: counting, graphing, making comparisons, visual discrimination

Now let's make a graph of the happy and sad faces you counted. The first row has been done for you. A happy face and a sad face have been drawn in. Fill in the other rows to complete the graph.

column 1   column 2

Here are two clues:
5 faces are happy
and 4 faces are sad.

How many 😊's
did you fill in? _____

How many 🙁's?
did you fill in? _____

Congratulations! You
have made a graph.

row 5

row 4

row 3

row 2

row 1

It's a birthday party! There are lots of good foods to eat. Do you see all the different foods?

How many *different kinds* of food are there? _____
Which ones are your favorites? _____

Now count up all the foods you see!

How many 's are there above? _____
How many 's did you count? _____
How many 's did you see? _____
How many 's are there in all? _____

Skills: counting, graphing, making comparisons, visual discrimination

You can make a graph of the birthday party foods. Use the number of each food you counted to fill in your graph. Draw the pictures in the correct columns. (The first row has been done for you.)

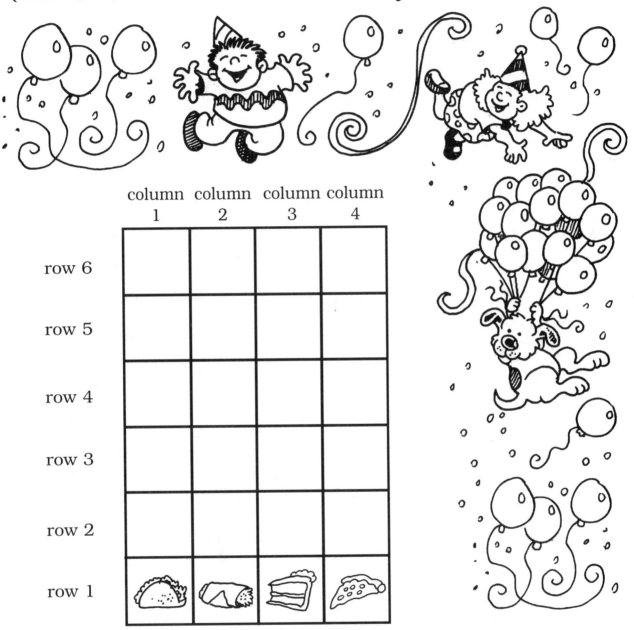

Which column has more? Circle one:

Which column has less? Circle one:

In which column is your favorite food? Column ____

Graphing

What yummy cookies! They are in the shape of four different animals. Before you count them, guess how many animals there are in all: _____

Now count up the animal cookies!
How many 🦒's did you count? _____
    How many 🐨's are there in all? _____
        What about 🐢's? How many are there? _____
            How many 🐎's do you see? _____

Skills: estimating, counting, graphing, making comparisons, visual discrimination

This graph is turned a different way! But you can still use it to show how many different cookies there are in the jar. Use the number of each animal you counted to fill in the rows with the missing pictures of 's and 🐑's. (The 🦒's and 🐻's are filled in for you.)

Which animal cookie is there the most of? _____
Which animal cookie is there the least of? _____
Two kinds of cookies have the same amount.
How many are there? _____

LET'S REVIEW

How much do you think you have learned about making graphs? Take this little test and see. Start by taking a good look at the creatures below.

1. How many creatures have 1 leg? ____   2 legs? ____

2. What about 3 legs? ____   4 legs? ____   5 legs? ____

3. Now fill in your graph. Zem-Zem is filled in for you.

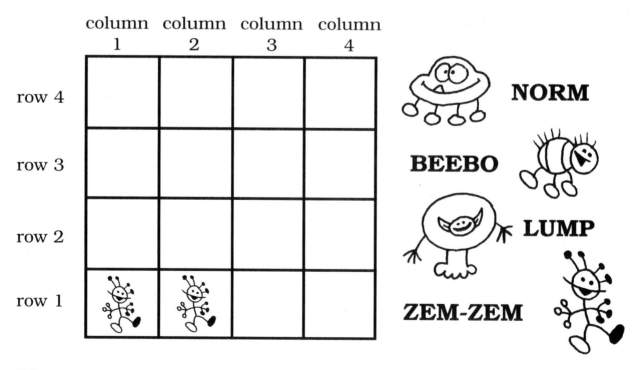

Skills: counting, graphing, visual discrimination

This Special Math Award Goes to:

_____
(my name)

I Can Graph ANYTHING!

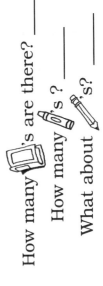

How many 's are there? _____
How many 🖍's ? _____
What about ✏'s? _____

books   crayons   pencils

MY NEW MATH WORDS:
About Time

daytime	minutes
clock	seconds
time	stopwatch
nighttime	midnight
first	noon
last	A.M.
wristwatch	P.M.

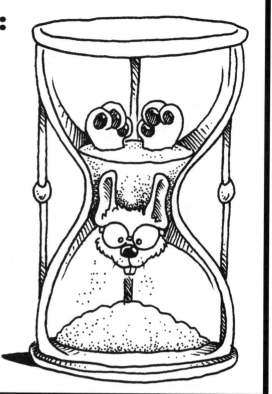

MY OLD MATH WORDS

There are too many old math words below! Connect the right ones with the pictures they belong to.

up

row

across

column

graph

Skills: math literacy, vocabulary building, discrimination, graphing skills

Roland Rooster likes the **daytime**, when the sun is bright and warm. Draw a line from the sun to all the daytime activities you see.

TOGETHER TIME! Here's how you can make your own **clock** to tell **time**. Copy this clock face on a piece of cardboard. You can make it as large as you want. Then cut out 2 clock hands, as shown. Ask an adult to push a fastener through the 2 hands in the middle of the clock face, and you're through!

IT'S EIGHT O'CLOCK!

Skills: times of the day, inference, deduction, sequencing time activities

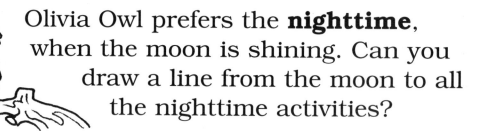

Olivia Owl prefers the **nighttime**, when the moon is shining. Can you draw a line from the moon to all the nighttime activities?

GRADE BOOSTER!

1

Put a ☆ next to the activities above (and on page 55, too) that can be done during the daytime or nighttime. Now make a list of some things you do during the day or the night.

Skills: times of the day, inference, deduction, sequencing activities by time

Can you put these pictures in order? Which comes **first**? Which comes **last**? Mark an X next to the picture that happens first. Circle the picture that happens last.

GRADE BOOSTER!

Look at each of the pictures above. Which activities take a long time to do? Write an "L" next to these. Which ones take a short time to do? Write an "S" next to these.

Time

Wendy the Walrus loves collecting **wristwatches** to tell time! Look at the activities listed below. Each one goes with a wristwatch. Help Wendy decide which activity goes where. The first one is done for you!

eating my lunch   going to school   doing my homework

✓ waking up   playing after school   eating my breakfast

waking up

_____

_____

_____

58   Skills: times of the day, sequencing activities by time, reading clock time, identification

TOGETHER TIME! Ask your mom, dad, or other adult to help you count how many **minutes** or **seconds** it takes you to do these fun activities. Hint: The best way to time yourself is with a **stopwatch**. A stopwatch measures how long it takes between the "start" and "end" of an activity. If you don't have a stopwatch, use a wristwatch or clock instead! (Remember: 60 seconds equals 1 minute.)

TIME
minutes   seconds

1. Brushing your teeth: _____ _____

2. Buttoning your sweater: _____ _____

3. Eating an ice-cream cone: _____ _____

4. Drinking a glass of milk: _____ _____

5. Making your bed: _____ _____

6. Running from the kitchen
   to the living room: _____ _____

Which activity took the most time? _____

Which activity took the least? _____

When something happens between 12:00 **midnight** and 12:00 **noon**, we say it is **A.M.**

When something happens between 12:00 noon and 12:00 midnight, it is **P.M.**

midnight   noon
        12:00 A.M.

noon   midnight
        12:00 P.M.

When the clock says: , what two times is it? It is noon, or 12:00 __.__. It is midnight, or 12:00 __.__.

Billy says good-bye to his mom and dad at the airport. It is 9:00 A.M.

Billy flies away to see his grandma. It takes 4 hours.

What time is it when Billy sees his grandma? Fill in the clock hands.

       +   **4 hours**   =

9:00 A.M.   +   **4 hours**   =   _____ ___.___.

LET'S REVIEW

Play ball! This baseball game will test what you know about time *and* addition!

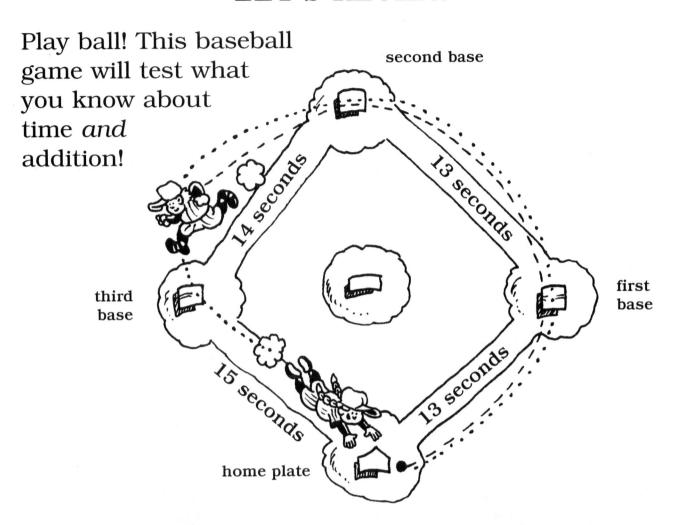

second base

13 seconds

14 seconds

first base

third base

15 seconds

13 seconds

home plate

1. Samuel hits the ball and makes it all the way to third base! How long does it take him to get there? (Note: seconds = sec.)

____ sec   +   ____ sec   +   ____ sec   =   ____ sec
(to first base)   (to second base)   (to third base)

2. Jenny hits a home run! How long does it take her to run all the bases and reach home plate?

____ sec + ____ sec + ____ sec + ____ sec = ____ sec
(to first base)   (to second base)   (to third base)   (to home plate)

Skills: time, addition, word problems

_____
(my name)

Is Right on Time
with Mathematics!

What time does the bear eat honey? _____ ___.___.
When does the mother bird feed her young? _____ ___.___.
What time is it when the giraffe has dinner? _____ ___.___.
When does the horse have breakfast? _____ ___.___.

CERTIFICATE OF COMPLETION

and Special Secret Message
especially for:

_____
(my name)

1	2	3	4	5	6	7	8	9	10	11	12
H	C	E	F	I	M	N	R	S	T	U	A

Each boxed number has a letter that goes with it. Put these letters in the blanks below to reveal the message. The first blank has been filled in for you!

I ___ ___ ___ ___ ___ ___ ___ ___ ___ ___
5 12   6   10   3   8   8   5   4   5   2

___ ___   ___ ___ ___ ___ !
5   7   6   12   10   1

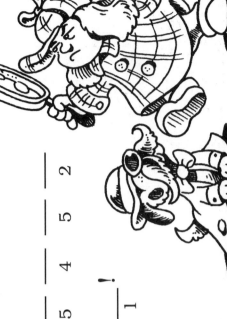
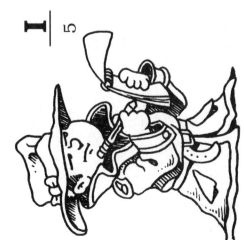

ANSWERS TO REVIEW TESTS

page 15

1. Snappy has 3 🍋's.
Squiggly has 5 🍋's.
5 > 3.

2. Snappy has 3 🍃's.
Squiggly has 2 🍃's.
2 < 3.

3. Snappy's total: 6.
Squiggly's total: 7.
7 > 6   *or*   6 < 7.

page 29

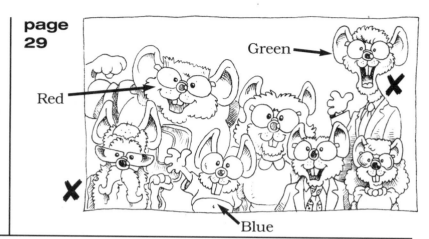

Green

Red

Blue

page 42

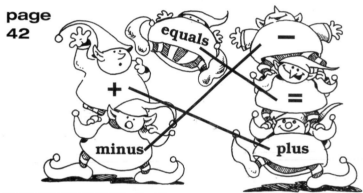

5	+	1	=	6
5	+	1	=	6
3	−	2	=	1
5	−	4	=	1
8	+	2	=	10

page 52

1. Two creatures have 1 leg.
Two creatures have 2 legs.

2. Three creatures have 3 legs.
Four creatures have 4 legs.
Zero creatures have 5 legs.

3.

	column 1	column 2	column 3	column 4	
row 4	🛸	🛸	🛸	🛸	**Norm**
row 3	🐝	🐝	🐝		**Beebo**
row 2	🐦	🐦			**Lump**
row 1	🧸	🧸			**Zem-Zem**

page 61

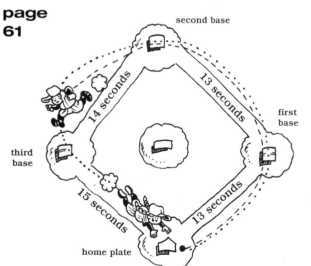

second base

first base

third base

home plate

14 seconds

13 seconds

15 seconds

13 seconds

1. It takes Samuel 40 seconds to reach third base.

13 sec + 13 sec + 14 sec = 40 sec

2. It takes Jenny 55 seconds to reach home plate.

13 sec + 13 sec + 14 sec + 15 sec = 55 sec

64